Energy Choices

Solar Energy

Julie Richards

Marshall Cavendish
Benchmark
New York

This edition first published in 2010 in the United States of America
by Marshall Cavendish Benchmark.

Marshall Cavendish Benchmark
99 White Plains Road
Tarrytown, NY 10591
www.marshallcavendish.us

All Internet sites were available and accurate when sent to press.

First published in 2009 by
MACMILLAN EDUCATION AUSTRALIA PTY LTD
15–19 Claremont Street, South Yarra 3141

Visit our website at www.macmillan.com.au or go directly to www.macmillanlibrary.com.au

Associated companies and representatives throughout the world.

Library of Congress Cataloging-in-Publication Data

Richards, Julie.
   Solar energy / by Julie Richards.
      p. cm. – (Energy choices)
   Includes index.
   ISBN 978-0-7614-4427-5
   1. Solar energy–Juvenile literature. I. Title.
   TJ810.3.R5 2009
   333.792'3–dc22
                              2009005909

Text and cover design by Christine Deering
Page layout by Domenic Lauricella
Photo research by Legend Images
Illustrations by Richard Morden

Printed in the United States

Acknowledgments

The author and the publisher are grateful to the following for permission to reproduce copyright material:

Front cover photograph: Solar power station, Australia courtesy of Photolibrary /John Mead/SPL

Photos courtesy of:
123rf/Leszek Scholz, 11 (top); AAP Image/Juan Ferreras, 26; AAP Image/Dean Lewins, 23; © Chiyacat/Dreamstime.com, 21;
© Christopher Elwell/Dreamstime.com, 18 (centre); © Kabby/Dreamstime.com, 25; © Qilux/Dreamstime.com, 18 (right);
Denis Doyle/Getty Images, 16; Mel Yates/Getty Images, 30; © Lena Andersson/iStockphoto, 12; © Robert Churchill/iStockphoto, 10
(left); © faberfoto_it/iStockphoto, 10 (right); © Nick Free/iStockphoto, 6; © Clayton Hansen/iStockphoto, 4 (top); © Justin Horrocks/
iStockphoto, 11 (bottom); © Daniel Stein/iStockphoto, 5; © Adam Tomasik/iStockphoto, 13; © Georg Winkens/iStockphoto, 14;
© Macquarie Generation, 17; NASA/JPL-Caltech, 24; NREL/DOE, photo by Mike Linenberger, 22; Photolibrary © Mark Boulton/
Alamy, 28; Photolibrary © P. Broze and A. Chederros, 8; Photolibrary © David Hancock/Alamy, 19; Photolibrary/Photo Researchers,
18 (top left); Photolibrary/Ralph Reinhold, 18 (bottom left); Photolibrary /John Mead/SPL, 1; Photolibrary/Hank Morgan/SPL, 15;
Sandia National Laboratory, 3, 27; Shutterstock, 29; © Petr Nad/Shutterstock, 20; © Jaimie D. Travis/Shutterstock, 4 (bottom).

While every care has been taken to trace and acknowledge copyright, the publisher tenders their apologies for any accidental
infringement where copyright has proved untraceable. Where the attempt has been unsuccessful, the publisher welcomes
information that would redress the situation.

135642

Contents

Glossary Words

When a word is printed in **bold**, you can look up its meaning in the Glossary on page 31.

What Is Energy?

Energy makes things work. Many machines need electrical energy to work. The more machines we use, the more electrical energy, or **electricity**, we need. Electrical energy is made in power stations.

toaster

laptop computer

These machines use electricity from a power station.

Most of the energy we use is made by burning **fossil fuels**, such as coal. Fossil fuels are running out because we use them too much. We need to use other sources to make **alternative energy**.

Burning fossil fuels releases pollution into the air.

Renewable Energy

Energy sources that will not run out are called renewable sources. Energy sources that will run out are called nonrenewable sources. Fossil fuels are a nonrenewable energy source.

The Sun is a renewable energy source.

Sustainable Energy

Sustainable energy is made from renewable energy sources. These sources will still be available in the future. They will not run out.

Comparing Energy Sources		
Energy Source	Renewable	Sustainable
Solar energy	✔	✔
Wind energy	✔	✔
Water energy	✔	✔
Nuclear energy	✘	✘
Biofuels	✔	✔
Fossil fuels	✘	✘

Solar Energy

Energy that comes from the Sun is called solar energy. Solar energy is a renewable energy source.

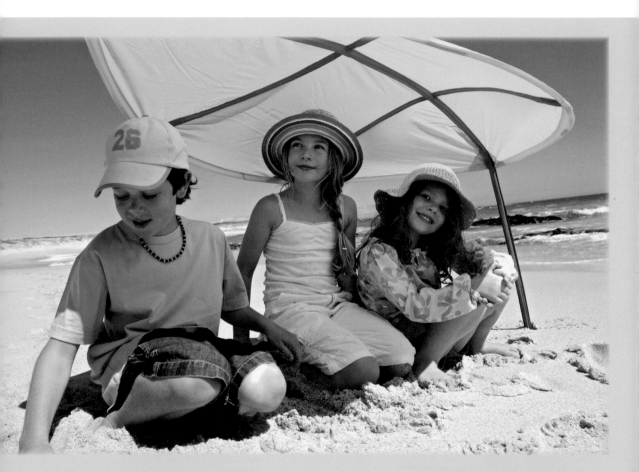

You can see solar energy as sunshine and feel it as heat.

The Sun makes solar energy. Although the Sun is far away, its energy travels quickly through space to Earth.

Gases in the Sun cause huge explosions.

Each explosion sends light and heat into space.

The light and heat travel in waves.

The Sun's energy brings light and heat to Earth.

Solar Energy in Nature

Natural solar energy warms Earth and gives us sunlight. Natural solar energy:

- helps plants to grow

- makes flowers open

- ripens fruits

Plants need sunlight to survive.

Natural solar energy heats Earth's deserts.

People use natural solar energy to dry their washing on a clothesline. Natural solar energy can be used in buildings and houses to help light and heat them.

Wet clothes dry quickly on a sunny day.

Skylights let light into rooms where there are no windows.

Making Electricity

Solar energy can be turned into electricity. Solar cells **absorb** the Sun's energy and use it to make electricity. The electricity is used right away or stored in a **battery**.

The sunnier it is, the more solar energy will be absorbed by this solar cell.

Many solar cells can be joined together to make a solar panel. Solar panels can be placed wherever they are needed.

Solar panels can be placed on the roof of a house.

Solar Farms

Solar farms have thousands of solar panels tilted toward the Sun. The panels absorb energy from the Sun.

Solar farms need a lot of space for all the solar panels.

Some solar farms are built in deserts. Deserts have little or no rain, so there are fewer clouds to block the Sun's energy.

Deserts are a perfect environment for solar farms.

Solar Power Stations

Some power stations use a solar power tower.
Mirrors reflect and focus sunlight onto the
tower. The energy is collected to make electricity.

reflected
sunlight

mirrors

This solar power tower in Spain uses 624 mirrors
to reflect sunlight.

Sometimes solar power stations are built next to coal-fired power stations. The solar power station can create electricity when it is sunny.

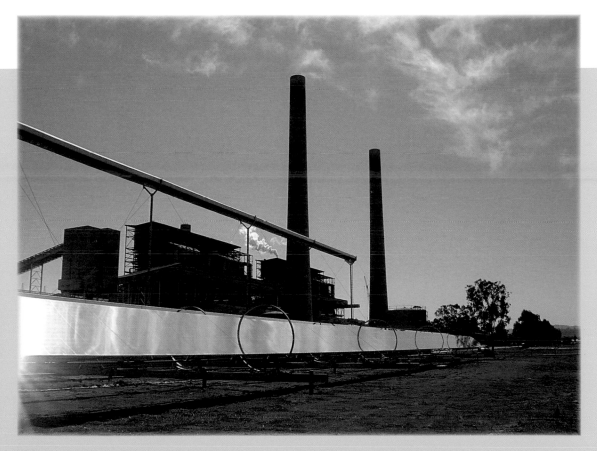

The coal-fired power station can create electricity on cloudy days.

Using Solar Energy

Solar energy can be used to power many things at home. Calculators, flashlights, radios, and even toys can use solar energy.

solar-powered radio

solar-powered calculator

solar-powered toy car

solar-powered battery charger

There are many solar-powered things that can be used at home.

Solar energy can be used to heat swimming pools and greenhouses. Solar lights can be used near garden paths and driveways.

This street light absorbs and stores solar energy during the day and lights up at night.

Solar Energy at Home

Solar energy can be used to heat water at home. The water runs slowly through the pipes inside a solar water heater and heats up. The hot water is stored in a tank for showers and baths.

Rooftop solar panels are used to heat water for this house.

Solar energy can also be used to make electricity in the home. When the Sun is not shining, electricity from other sources is used instead.

These rooftop solar panels, made up of many solar cells, turn sunshine into electricity.

Solar-powered Transportation

Solar energy can be used for transportation. Solar cells can power small cars that do not need to travel very far.

solar panels

This car can recharge its battery using solar energy.

Solar-powered boats have solar panels to absorb the Sun's energy from the sky. The panels also absorb energy from sunlight reflected off the water.

Solar panels power this passenger ferry.

Solar Energy in Remote Places

Solar energy powers equipment used in spacecraft and **satellites**. Remote-controlled robots are also powered by solar energy. They explore planets to which humans cannot travel.

This solar-powered robot explored the planet Mars.

Solar energy is useful in mountainous areas or deserts. It is too expensive and difficult to build coal-fired power stations in these **remote** environments.

In remote places, solar energy can power equipment such as this solar light.

The Future of Solar Energy

Scientists are working on ways to make solar energy cheap enough for everyone. This will help **conserve** the world's energy sources.

Solar dishes like this can be used for cooking.

A large solar farm is being built in the desert in the United States. Solar dishes will reflect the Sun's energy onto engines to make electricity. This solar farm will be the world's largest solar energy system.

These solar dishes follow the Sun as it moves across the sky.

Using Less Energy

Using less energy will conserve energy sources and reduce pollution. Buying **appliances** that are **energy-efficient** is one way to use less energy in the home.

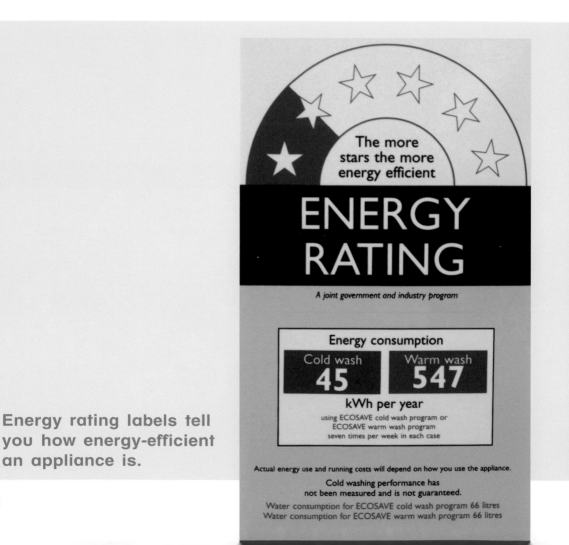

Energy rating labels tell you how energy-efficient an appliance is.

The more stars the more energy efficient

ENERGY RATING

A joint government and industry program

Energy consumption

Cold wash	Warm wash
45	547

kWh per year

using ECOSAVE cold wash program or
ECOSAVE warm wash program
seven times per week in each case

Actual energy use and running costs will depend on how you use the appliance.

Cold washing performance has
not been measured and is not guaranteed.

Water consumption for ECOSAVE cold wash program 66 litres
Water consumption for ECOSAVE warm wash program 66 litres

Today, many things are made to use less electricity than in the past.

Low-energy lightbulbs do not use as much electricity as traditional lightbulbs.

How Can We Help?

Everybody can help the environment by using less energy. We can use less energy by:

- switching off lights and appliances when they are not being used

- asking for presents that do not use electricity to work

If you feel cold, put on a sweater instead of turning up the heater.

Glossary

absorb   Soak up.

alternative energy   Energy made from a source, such as the Sun, instead of from fossil fuels.

appliances   Machines, such as televisions, which need electricity to work.

battery   A container that stores energy.

conserve   Save.

electricity   Electrical energy that is carried along wires.

energy-efficient   Uses energy without waste.

fossil fuels   Coal, oil, and gas.

remote   A long way away from cities and difficult to get to.

satellites   Spacecraft that circle Earth.

Index